The Manitoba Landscape

A VISUAL SYMPHONY

The Manitoba Landscape

A VISUAL SYMPHONY

Photography and text by Robert R. Taylor
Windermere House Publishing

Published by
Windermere House Publishing
944 Windermere Ave.
Winnipeg, Manitoba
R3T 1A1

ISBN. 1-550-56-021-2
First Edition
Copyright ©1990 — Robert R. Taylor

Book design by Steve Penner
Printed and bound in Canada by
DW Friesen
Altona, Manitoba, Canada
R0G 0B0

Title page –
Beautiful displays of wildflowers can be found in natural areas throughout the province during the summer months. This is Arnica and Hedysarum at Churchill.

▶ *A clump of birch accents the autumn colours of the Belair Provincial Forest near Stead.*

Big Bluestem, a native prairie grass, sometimes grows to a height of six feet. Tall-grass prairie once covered much of southeastern Manitoba. Today only a few small scattered remnants remain.

D E D I C A T I O N

....

I would like to dedicate
THE MANITOBA LANDSCAPE: A Visual Symphony
to my parents, Ross and Alice Taylor,
who always supported and encouraged my
interests in nature and art.

ACKNOWLEDGEMENTS

· ·

I am most grateful for the support, advice, and encouragement of many of my friends and acquaintances. There are the companions who have shared field trips: Paul Guyot, who loved life and nature and who lived zestfully to the end, Bob Pollock, Glenn Moncrieff, Peter Sawatzky, Dennis Fast and Dave and Joan Dyson, with whom I have travelled many miles of Manitoba roads, in search of photographs.

Dr. Robert Nero has not only been a frequent companion in the field, but has also given much encouragement and editorial advice. His knowledge of the province and its natural history is an invaluable resource.

My thanks also to John Oleksiuk who has given me valued assistance and advice on production and marketing. Walter Kaiser and his staff at Custom Images photo lab have done a fine job on preparing some of the photographs for reproduction.

I am appreciative of the contribution made by David G. Friesen and his capable staff at DW Friesen in Altona, Manitoba, who were always helpful and very professional. My greatest debt of gratitude goes to Steve Penner at Friesens who did the excellent design, helped me to select the images, and discussed every last detail of the production with me to get the best possible end result.

There are numerous others who helped me through this project in countless ways. They are all important and appreciated.

Aspen forest, such as this patch near Turtle Mountain Provincial Park, is a familiar part of the Manitoba scene.

A resplendent patch of Purple Saxifrage flourishes in the midst of a gravel esker near Churchill.

INTRODUCTION

· ·

*T*hose who were born and raised in Manitoba have an attachment to the place which can never be denied. This is their home, their place of origin. Others have come to live here from all corners of the world bringing with them traditions and artistic expressions which have combined to weave a rich cultural mosaic.

Even the landscape has been influenced in various ways by the diversity of new settlers to Manitoba. Some came as fishermen, some worked the forests, while others developed farms of different types. Still others ventured into remote parts of the province to build homesteads and to earn a living from the land in more obscure ways.

The landscape of Manitoba is as diverse and fascinating as the people who came to live here. Local features and variations are endless, favourite places of those who discover them. Then there are the details, the trees, wildflowers, fields, meadows, birds, mammals, and other creatures which have their niches in our land. It all fits together in a grand and intricate way.

We have material for a lifetime of discovery in our own backyard. We have only to get out and wander around Manitoba, to open our eyes and appreciate the beauty of this place which we call home.

Living in Manitoba has given me a wealth of opportunities to explore and enjoy. Within the pages of this volume are some of the wonderful scenes and subjects which I have been privileged to observe. I hope that I can convey some of these experiences to you through my photographs and that you will be inspired to seek out some of these special places for yourself.

F O R E W O R D

. . . .

A land of diversity where one can saunter through rolling sand dunes, paddle upon remote wilderness lakes, explore the shoreline of an Arctic sea, or motor through a vast network of country roads; that is Manitoba.

There are many unique features contained within these provincial boundaries. Some are obvious and spectacular, some are subtle and obscure. Ancient glaciers have played a major role here in shaping the land, leaving us with two of the largest freshwater lakes in the world and many smaller ones.

A wide variety of soil types nourish a great diversity of plant life, both wild and domestic. Scattered across the breadth of Manitoba are extensive deposits of sand and gravel. Rich clay soil and sandy loam have determined the regions of farming. Much peat bog, with accompanying Black Spruce and Tamarack, is found from the southeast to the northwest. And there is the underlying bedrock which surfaces in many places giving a sense of geological history and stability.

In Manitoba there are thousands of acres of forest of various types, interspersed in the south and west with farmlands yielding crops and livestock of many kinds. There are a few small remnants of the tall-grass prairie which covered much of the southeast in the past, and some mixed-grass prairie with its shorter grasses and sage. Aspen parkland occupies much of the southern half of the province, gradually blending into the boreal forest in mixtures of various proportions. The northern forest diminishes toward the muskeg and old beach ridges of the Hudson Bay lowlands and the subarctic tundra of the northwest. The coast of Hudson Bay itself is a fine arctic marine habitat.

Climate and the seasons are a major influence on life in Manitoba. Vegetation types and growth rates, wildlife activities and migrations, and the lives of Manitobans are governed to a great extent by climatological factors. Summer days are long, winter days are short. Spring and autumn are times of rapid change. There are major events in the weather conditions here; the late afternoon thunderstorms of a hot summer day, the occasional fearsome tornado, and a good old-fashioned blizzard now and then. These are spectacles which can humble even the most arrogant and help to build the strength of character and self-reliance attributable to so many Canadians.

The sun shines in Manitoba more often than in most other parts of Canada. In summer we enjoy its warmth as we participate in all sorts of outdoor activities. The springtime sun activates the juices of life within a myriad of plants and unlocks the earth from the icy grip of winter. The autumn sun plays harmoniously on the colourful palette of the changing landscape. And those cold, cold winter days. Who can forget the exhilaration of the low winter sun on a windless day, and those crisp blue skies.

There are details in the Manitoba landscape. Often they are overlooked, or appreciated only by poets, painters, and the like. A unique rock formation, natural sculpting of ice, ripples in a sand dune, a design of lichens on a bedrock background, or a beautiful roadside flower; they are all present in Manitoba, in profusion. They are there for the looking, if one takes the time and makes the effort.

The natural curiosity which we have as children seems to be overwhelmed by other factors in our lives as we gain a formal education, develop daily routines, establish social and family relationships, and become employed in our choice of career.

Within the pages of this book I hope that I can provide some insight into the landscape of Manitoba, its various moods and compositions, and some of its component details. Perhaps you will develop a greater understanding of the role which light plays upon the land and of the joys of the changing seasons. With some effort you could train yourself to be more observant and more appreciative of the passing landscape as you traverse the roads and paths of this fascinating province. And perhaps, with this new appreciation for the beauty and fragility of our landscape, you will become committed to taking better care of our land, air, and water.

HOW TO USE THIS BOOK

....

*I*t is my sincere hope that you will not just flip quickly through the pages of this Manitoba Landscape book then leave it neglected somewhere on a coffee table or bookshelf. I had many years of enjoyable experiences in the field making the photographs for the book and it is my intention to try to convey some of those special moments and places to you.

So I suggest that you take an hour once in a while, put on some soft instrumental music, relax in your favourite chair, and lose yourself in these pages.

Study the photographs carefully. Look for tiny details. Appreciate the quality and direction of light. Pretend that you are there on location. Feel the wind in your hair, the sun on your face, or the appropriate temperature. Imagine the sounds that you would hear as you observe the scene. Let yourself become absorbed in the total experience which you and the photograph fashion together.

This lyrical fencepost composition, near Marquette, stands in silent tribute to the hand which fashioned it many years ago.

The long days of summer yield a midnight sunset beyond dead spruce spires near the Hudson Bay shore.

A Visual Symphony

Tuning in to the land generates a harmony within me.
The wind whispers a peaceful acceptance of my presence
While the crystal offerings of a horned lark
Play above the rhythms of a furrowed field.
In another place, black spruce spires
Rise against the muted tones of an evening sky.
Along the lake, gently lapping waters
Bathe shoreline boulders in reflected light.
Myriads of stimuli
Combine in orchestration of a varied landscape,
A visual symphony
For the appreciative eye.

Robert R. Taylor

The small owls are widely distributed but seldom seen because of their nocturnal habits.
These young Saw-whet Owls have just left the security of their tree-cavity nest.

The Manitoba Landscape

A V I S U A L S Y M P H O N Y

land-scape / lan(d)-,skāp / n 1: a picture representing a view of natural inland scenery 2: a portion of land that the eye can see in one glance

*Sage is often found in abundance in pastures of
the southwest near Lyleton and Tilston.*

Sometimes as they come into view the delicate blue flowers of a Flax field give the appearance of a body of water.

*A passing summer storm releases the evening sun to play upon
the golden tones of a ripened crop south of Glenboro.*

The brilliant yellow of a blossoming Canola field dominates the scene near Underhill.

▲ *A light spring rain stimulates growth in pastures throughout the province such as this one on Highway 10 south of Brandon.*
▶ *A barbed-wire fence divides pasture from sunflower near Snowflake.*

▲ *Swaths of golden-brown Buckwheat lie waiting for the combine southwest of Morden.*

▶ *A swather makes its rounds in view of the Goodlands elevator.*

▲ *The valley road west of Roseisle is a peaceful place for an autumn stroll.*

▶ *Aglow with colour, the Pembina River valley winds its way through south-central Manitoba.*

The warm spring sun begins to unlock the dormant energies of the Souris River valley.

In mid-April the Prairie Crocus, floral emblem of Manitoba, emerges from southern soils to greet spring.

The ''Spirit Sands'' in Spruce Woods Provincial Park move with the prevailing
wind. The leading edge of a dune flows over everything in its path.

Ripples of sand characterize the open dunes of the hills between Carberry and Glenboro.

▲ *A cultivated field north of Fannystelle plays host to a wintering Snowy Owl.*

▶ *One of the ultimate winter pleasures is cross-country skiing in the Spruce Woods area northwest of Holland.*

Many stories have echoed in the walls of abandoned farmhouses such as this one near Coulter.

Cattle graze peacefully in the warm evening light of summer along Hwy. 5, north of Belmont.

▲ *Vivid colours dominate the landscape after a late summer storm near Elm Creek.*

▶ *The Assiniboine River winds its way across western Manitoba. The sunset sky north of Alexander portrays the scene in the simplest of forms.*

Transitional bands of vegetation define the edge of the Delta Marsh, one of the best known wetlands in North America.

The rattling song of the Marsh Wren can be heard in healthy marsh habitat across the southern half of the province.

*Phragmites, or giant reed grass, is silhouetted in the shallows
of Lake Manitoba between Delta Beach and Lynch Point.*

In the Lake Manitoba marshes near Oak Point, Giant Canada Geese arrive at their overnight roosting ponds.

*Post-glacial lakes and ponds known as "potholes" are an intricate feature of the landscape
in the Minnedosa area. They are extremely important waterfowl breeding grounds.*

A view of the Little Saskatchewan River west of Minnedosa shows a variety of features.

▲ *Raw simplicity in a prairie landscape, an old farmhouse near Rackham.*

▶ *Rising as a giant monolith from the flat plains below, Riding Mountain can be seen from a great distance; Hwy. 10 near Dauphin.*

*Many backcountry roads around Riding Mountain yield
treasured little scenes such as this one west of Onanole.*

Aspen leaves descend upon a layer of autumn snow along a trail in Riding Mountain.

The ethereal magentas of a winter evening provide a stage for a pair of sturdy Bur Oaks, near Kleefeld.

A dramatic winter afternoon north of Inwood.

▲ *Frost-covered grasses arch across a field near Headingley while "Sundogs" hang in the sky beyond.*

▶ *A spectacular sun circle with "Sundogs" looms above the Red River in Winnipeg's Crescent Park.*

▲ *Some degree of flooding occurs each year along the Red River during spring break-up as seen from the bridge at Ste. Agathe.*

▶ *Near Selkirk and at other points along the Red River, early farms were established in long strips with narrow river frontage for access. These patterns can still be seen in many places.*

▲ *White-tailed Deer are common throughout the south. This doe and fawn were at the Fort Whyte Centre, Winnipeg.*
▶ *In many locations around the larger lakes and rivers White Pelicans are a unique and spectacular summer visitor.*

East Pine Creek, on Hwy. 12 in the Sandilands Provincial Forest, wanders off into a Tamarack bog.

Tamaracks throughout the province are turned to gold by the cold days of autumn.

A profusion of golden yellows signifies the final flourish of the rustling leaves of aspen.

Ruffed Grouse cruise the forest floor over a wide range. Their resonant "drumming" during spring courtship carries a great distance through the woods.

An exposition in pink,
evening clouds near Zhoda.

On a cool April night, Northern Lights dance above spruce spires near Marchand.

*The soft, plumed head of Phragmites glows
against an ominous autumn sky.*

A peaceful winter afternoon broken only by the occasional crunch of snowshoes upon the crusty surface, near Sprague.

▲ *There are many beautiful lakes in Manitoba, each with its own uniqueness. In the Whiteshell, these shield country lakes are particularly attractive.*

▶ *Watching a sunset through the pine branches is good for the soul. Many seek rejuvenation in the Whiteshell and other such places.*

The morning sun breaks across the Lily Pond on Hwy. 44.

White Water Lilies accent many ponds and bays throughout the summer.

*A cut-line through the forest demarcates the border between
Manitoba and Ontario at the Trans-Canada Highway.*

Gray Tree Frogs can change colour to match their surroundings. They can be heard calling throughout the southeast on spring and early summer nights.

◄ *The bright reds of Dwarf Sumach may be seen along the roadsides of the Whiteshell in the autumn.*

► *Bedrock of the Canadian Shield surfaces throughout much of the eastern side of the province and on into the north.*

◄ *Fascinating boulder arrangements called "mosaics" can be found in several locations in Whiteshell Provincial Park. They were created many years ago by native shamans.*

▶ *Pillows of lichen adorn the exposed bedrock along Hwy. 44 near Rennie.*

*The upper portion of Tulabi Falls
in Nopiming Provincial Park.*

Reeds accent the shallows at the east end of Bird Lake.

▲ *Tree silhouettes are mirrored in the glassy surface of a calm Nopiming Lake.*

▶ *Glaciation has played a major role in shaping the surface of Manitoba. We see the rounding effect on the shoreline rock of a small lake east of Tulabi Lake.*

▲ *Blueberries are abundant in old burn areas in years of adequate moisture.*

▶ *A barren landscape remains in the wake of an extensive forest fire in the Davidson Lake region.*

Great Gray Owls, the provincial bird emblem, can sometimes be seen hunting along roadsides in the eastern and northern regions during the winter. Lac du Bonnet is one of the favoured areas.

An overnight burrow or "kieppi" of a grouse features in the foreground of a Tamarack bog along the winter road to Island Lake.

▲ *The combination of fresh snow and some open water is particularly appealing as seen here on the Manigotogan River.*

▶ *"Jewels" of ice form intriguing patterns along the edge of moving waters during the winter.*

◄ *The vastness of Lake Winnipeg is apparent at sunrise near Berens River.*

▶ *Sand dunes are a dominant feature of the landscape at Grand Beach.*

A stark contrast as a Yellow Lady's Slipper blooms in the foreground of a recently burned forest near Ashern.

Yellow Lady's Slippers are seen along roadsides and in boggy areas during the month of June.

Charred trunks lend a touch of awesome beauty to the devastated forest beyond.

Fireweed proliferates in disturbed areas or after a forest fire.

▲ *Bunchberry is common in Duck Mountain Provincial Park and in other coniferous and mixed-forest areas of the province.*

▶ *Duck Mountain Provincial Park has many picturesque and accessible lakes which are ideal for a peaceful day of canoeing.*

The crystal waters of Clearwater Lake at The Pas seem more like a tropical paradise than northern Manitoba.

Limestone shelves around the shoreline give a unique character to Rocky Lake near Wanless.

▲ *Many of the inhabitants of our land live their lives in relative obscurity, unless perhaps their handiworks are highlighted by the morning sun.*

▶ *Morning dew turns a roadside meadow into a fantasyland of spider webs, grasses, and shrubs, north of The Pas.*

▲ *The call of the Common Loon is symbolic of wilderness. Many lakes in Manitoba provide nesting sites for this majestic bird. Large flocks of non-breeding loons congregate on lakes in the Flin Flon region in July and August.*

▶ *This forest south of Flin Flon takes on an ethereal quality in the mist of a summer morning.*

Wekusko Falls near Snow Lake is one of many picturesque waterfalls throughout the north.
Unlike many others, this one is accessible to highway travellers.

A small island in Snow Lake glows in the path of the evening sun.

◄ *Moss carpets the forest floor in a damp micro-climate near Pisew Falls.*

► *Remnants of the winter ice-bridge below Pisew Falls can be seen in this early June view.*

▲ *An aerial view of the northeastern tundra shows a profusion of lakes and ponds.*

▶ *Lichen-covered ridges interspersed with scattered spruce are prevalent southwest of York Factory.*

Tide-stranded ice sculptures line the shore of Hudson Bay in June and early July, creating a magnificent gallery of frigid art.

Rounded pebbles on the Hudson Bay shore encroach upon the bedrock of blue quartzite. Glacial scratches on the surface are accented by the low evening light.

◀ *Cape Merry, a national historic site at the mouth of the Churchill River. Fort Prince of Wales is located on the west side of the river.*

▶ *A "popcorn" sky hangs above the boggy shore of a tundra lake near Churchill.*

*Willow catkins emerge
in June as spring comes
to the Churchill region.
Twenty-one species of
willow have been
identified in this area.*

A splendid display of colour dominates the tundra as the Rhododendron comes into bloom in mid-June.

▲ *The male Willow Ptarmigan retains some of the white winter colouration during the early nesting period. Along with his distinctive call it is used to distract intruders and lead them away from the nest site.*

▶ *Thousands of Canada Goose goslings are raised on the tundra each summer where conditions are ideal and food is plentiful.*

*Autumn colour comes to
the tundra in late August
or September as the
leaves of Bearberry,
Snow Willow, and many
others turn to crimson.*

Winter comes early to the north. Snow crystals carried on the wind accumulate around any obstacle, creating graceful patterns on the barren landscape.

▲ *Sparring Polar Bears at Gordon Point east of Churchill. Polar Bears attract visitors from around the world to Manitoba in the fall.*

▶ *Fog rolls in from Hudson Bay on a late October morning providing an unusual background for this juvenile Polar Bear.*

Enveloped in ice from a freezing rain, a willow glitters in an arctic sunset.

Along the marine coastline of Hudson Bay harsh winds inhibit the growth of branches on the north and west sides of the spruce trees, giving them a unique shape.

Great works of art
Are there for the seeing,
At our feet
And within our view,
A feast for the eye
That looks toward the land.